Little
Pebble™

Baby Animals and Th

BABY ANIMALS
In BURROWS

by Martha E. H. Rustad

CAPSTONE PRESS
a capstone imprint

Little Pebble is published by Capstone Press,
1710 Roe Crest Drive, North Mankato, Minnesota 56003
www.mycapstone.com

Library of Congress Cataloging-in-Publication Data
Names: Rustad, Martha E. H. (Martha Elizabeth Hillman), 1975- author.
Title: Baby animals in burrows / by Martha E.H. Rustad.
Description: North Mankato, Minnesota : Capstone Press, [2017] | Series:
     Little pebble. Baby animals and their homes | Audience: Ages 4-8. |
Audience: K to grade 3. | Includes bibliographical references and index.
Identifiers: LCCN 2016031957| ISBN 9781515738312 (library binding)
     ISBN 9781515738350 (pbk.) | ISBN 9781515738473 (ebook pdf)
Subjects: LCSH: Animals—Habitations—Juvenile literature. |
     Animals—Infancy—Juvenile literature.
Classification: LCC QL756.15 .R86 2017 | DDC 591.56/4—dc23
LC record available at https://lccn.loc.gov/2016031957

Editorial Credits
Carrie Braulick Sheely, editor; Juliette Peters, designer;
Tracey Engel, media researcher; Katy LaVigne, production specialist

Photo Credits
Alamy: Mark Colombus, 7, NatPar Collection, 20–21; Minden Pictures: Konrad Wothe, 19;
Na-ture in Stock/Ronald Stiefelhagen, 9; Shutterstock: Henk Bentlage, 13, 15, HHsu, 11,
ifong, Back Cover and Design Element, Michael C. Gray, Front Cover, Ondrej Prosicky, 3
Bottom Left, sittipong, Back Cover Design Element, Vladimir Wrangel, 5, Volodymyr Burdiak,
1 Bot-tom Left, Waddell Images, 17

Table of Contents

Burrow Babies

Some baby animals
grow up in burrows.
Burrows are
under the ground.

A puffin chick lives in the back of a burrow. **Cheep!** Its parents feed it fish.

Zzz.

A badger cub sleeps.

It wakes up.

It drinks milk from mom.

Bunnies need a home.

A rabbit digs a burrow.

She lines it with fur.

Up and Down

Prairie dog burrows are big.

Pups grow in one room.

They come up to play.

Baby meerkats look out.

Bark!

Mom warns her pups.

They go back down.

A baby armadillo
looks for food.
Mom helps.
They find bugs.
They go back in their burrow.

A trap door spider looks out.

A bird!

She closes the door.

Her babies stay safe.

Eggs lie in a burrow.

Crack!

Baby desert tortoises
crawl out. Hello!

Glossary

armadillo—a desert animal with bony plates covering its body

burrow—a hole in the ground made or used by an animal

parent—a mother or a father

tortoise—a reptile with a hard shell

warn—to tell about a danger that might happen

Read More

Chung, Liz. *Inside Rabbit Burrows*. Inside Animal Homes. New York: PowerKids Press, 2016.

Gish, Melissa. *Armadillos*. Living Wild. Mankato, Minn.: Creative Education, 2016.

Royston, Angela. *Animals That Dig*. Adapted to Survive. Chicago: Capstone Raintree, 2014.

Internet Sites

FactHound offers a safe, fun way to find Internet sites related to this book. All of the sites on FactHound have been researched by our staff.

Here's all you do:
Visit *www.facthound.com*
Type in this code: 9781515738312

Super-cool stuff!

Check out projects, games and lots more at
www.capstonekids.com

Critical Thinking Using the Common Core

1. How do burrows help keep baby animals safe? (Integration of Knowledge and Ideas)

2. Look at the photo on page 17. How do you think the bony plates on the armadillos help protect them? (Craft and Structure)

Index